Emma (

Verbally Abusive Relationships:

No more suffering!

A how to Prevent & Save guide.

Verbal Abuse in Couples

Verbally Abusive Relationships: No more suffering! A how to Prevent & Save guide.

Domestic abuse is a term that is familiar to most. Another term commonly used in the same context is couples' violence. This term lends a strong connotation to physical abuse, which is a very serious form of abuse but is not the only kind.

Another equally important kind of abuse is emotional abuse, which includes verbal abuse. Emotional abuse is when one or both partners treat the other in emotionally damaging, neglectful, controlling, or manipulative ways. While some may make an effort to diminish its significance, emotional abuse is a real and very serious type of abuse. Victims of emotional abuse often find themselves isolated and hesitant to confide their experiences in other people. A specific area of emotional abuse is verbal abuse.

Verbal abuse is not something to be taken lightly. Although many abusers themselves, even high profile ones, try to undermine the severity of this form of abuse, it cannot be undermined. Various studies in recent years have highlighted and proven the fact that verbal abuse produces the same psychological effects, sometimes worse and longer lasting effects, as physical abuse. This is a phenomenon to pay attention to and to face head on.

The identifiable types of verbal abuse must be taught widely to people of all ages, in order to prevent victims suffering without need. It is important that all people be aware of what verbal abuse is. That's why I wrote this book in the first place – to teach you how to recognize Verbal abuse, how to prevent you or someone from abusing others and how to help those were abused. That's why you should read this book in the first place – to help yourself and your loved ones. Don't suffer! Don't abuse! Read this book and begin a new life!

Abuse of a Different Nature

Domestic abuse is a term that is familiar to most. It is often used in the media referring to abusive situations within couples. Another term commonly used in the same context is couples' violence. This term lends a strong connotation to physical abuse, which is a very serious form of abuse, but it's not the only kind.

Another equally important kind of abuse is emotional abuse, which includes verbal abuse. Emotional abuse is when one or both partners treat the other in emotionally damaging, neglectful, controlling, or manipulative ways. This type of abuse has a grave effect on the psychological wellbeing of the victim. Verbal abuse is one of the main types of emotional abuse, which has many subtypes of its own. Emotional and verbal abuse can feel elusive or abstract to some, which can make it difficult for victims to express themselves clearly.

While some may make an effort to diminish its significance, emotional abuse is a real and very serious type of abuse. Victims of emotional abuse often find themselves isolated and hesitant to confide their experiences in other people. The abuser has usually managed to create a feeling within the victim that they are unworthy of better treatment, or that they deserve to be abused. It is essential that victims of emotional abuse learn that they are, in fact, experiencing something damaging and that their suffering is recognized. Victims of emotional abuse need to be supported.

A specific area of emotional abuse is verbal abuse. It can sometimes feel confusing to be able to determine when one is being verbally abused. Throughout different cultures, varying levels of acceptance are exercised in terms of the way in which couples speak to each other. There are, however, certain verbal patterns and behaviors that are abusive no matter what cultural standards proclaim. There are no cultural exceptions for verbal or emotional abuse, and this must be understood by all, especially victims seeking information and help.

The Abusers

Verbal abuse is never the victim's 'fault.' This is something that the abuser often works hard to make the victim believe but is never true. So how do the abusers manage to make their victims feel responsible for what they are experiencing? This is a result of intricate manipulation.

People do not enter relationships with other people if they know that they will be abused. This is what is difficult about verbal abuse in couples. It often begins to the complete surprise of the victim. Many people who turn out to be abusers in their relationships exhibit no signs of this in the courting process. In fact, they may even be aware of what they are doing, and purposely work to make sure that the victim grows to trust them and even love them before beginning their abuse.

Usually, during the time when a couple is getting to know each other, the abuser appears and behaves in the complete opposite way. Abuse from this person would never trust the victim's mind. The abuser appears open and interested in all the victim thinks and wants to say. They are supportive and go out of their way to help the victim. They tell their victims that they like everything about them, and maybe even that they have never felt this way. Victims of verbal and emotional abuse are often wooed very quickly and promised exactly what they have been dreaming of in a relationship. The abuser will do anything it takes to present this image of themselves to the victim, and to secure their faith.

Another important thing to know about abusers is that quite often, even their closest friends and family are not aware of their capacity for abuse. A victim of future abuse may meet the abuser's friends and family early in the relationship. It is likely that the abuser's friends and family will talk about what a great person the abuser is, and it will appear that the abuser is a very well-rounded person with excellent relationships. The reality, however, is usually that the other people in the abuser's life do not know about their abusive capacities because they have never been a victim of the abuser themselves.

The beginning of any relationship with an abuser is carefully crafted to appear as the relationship of the victim's dreams. As they are falling deeper and deeper in love with the abuser, the victim is unknowingly compromising their ability to distinguish abusive behaviors and words from their partner. The abuser purposely secures a deep level of intimacy before they allow themselves to show any sign of abuse towards the victim. This is because they want to have full control of the relationship and its standards.

Not all abusers are planning their manipulation and shift into abuse from the beginning of the relationship. There are many people who may not be aware of their own abusive capacities. Some abusers have grown up in environments where they were victims or witnesses to emotional and verbal abuse themselves. Often times, this may go unbeknownst to them because they learned that this was the norm within a relationship or family. These people often find themselves playing out the same roles that they experienced as children. This is not an excuse for their verbally and emotionally abusive behavior. These types of abusers must also take responsibility for their actions and seek professional help in order to learn how to function healthily in a partnership. Verbal and emotional abuse are never excusable behaviors.

So does the verbal abuse begin suddenly and intensely? It can, but often it creeps into the relationship without the victim's full awareness of what is happening. One day the victim may find themselves asking when their partner became so mean and hurtful, but it is likely that if they looked back in the relationship, they would see how the abuser began changing their behaviors.

The Subtle Beginning to Abuse

When the verbal and emotional abuse starts, the victim is usually caught off guard and finds themselves rationalizing the abuse. A relationship has been going just as a young woman had always dreamed. She and her boyfriend are able to talk about everything and anything, and often find themselves staying up all night discussing whatever comes to mind. They enjoy doing the same things and have fun going out with each other's friends. She feels supported and beautiful with her boyfriend and has grown to trust that he cares for her. She believes that she can always count on him for honesty, help, and care.

One night, as the couple is getting ready to go out for a night with his friends, the boyfriend tells his girlfriend that the dress she is wearing makes her look fat. The girlfriend feels a sharp pang in her chest, and her throat feels tight. She is surprised by this comment. Her boyfriend has never said anything about her clothes except how beautiful they are. She takes a breath and asks him what he means. He answers that she is so beautiful that he does not think she would want to go out with his friends wearing something that makes her look fat.

Slightly confused, but rushing to rationalize the situation for herself, the girlfriend tells herself that her boyfriend must be saying this because he cares about her. He does not want me to go out and be wrongly judged by others because of a bad dress, she thinks to herself. That's sweet of him. I'll change into that other dress that he really likes.

She changes into a dress that her boyfriend has always raved about. When she asks if she looks better, her boyfriend tells her it's acceptable. In one moment, he has changed the dynamic within the relationship. He has created a feeling of uncertainty in the victim's mind. Where she once felt confident and beautiful, the victim now feels like she must seek her boyfriend's approval about her clothes.

This is one example of how verbal abuse begins in a relationship. When the victim has grown to trust the abuser, they are quick and adept at rationalizing what they would recognize in others as abusive remarks and behaviors. Once the victim has confusedly accepted abuse, they have unwittingly approved a new, lower standard of respect from their partner, the abuser. After the initial introduction of verbal abuse, the victim will find that they are being abused increasingly in different areas of their relationship and life. By the time they recognize what is happening, the victim is caught in a complicated web of love and abuse that they cannot see how to navigate their way out of.

The Cycle of Abuse

After the initial introduction of abuse into a relationship, the abuser tends to recreate a pattern. The victim may or may not notice this pattern. However, even if they do notice the pattern, they will find that they are opposed by the abuser when they try to confront the relationship's unhealthy dynamic change. The abuser will often deny that any abuse has occurred and tell the victim that they are overreacting or that they are simply too sensitive. In this new state of confusion, the victim is likely to second-guess themselves and question whether they are in fact too sensitive or overreacting. Victims of verbal abuse are not too sensitive. They are not overreacting. They are being manipulated into losing trust in themselves, fostering a friendlier environment for the abuse.

The cycle of abuse is simple and concrete. There is an **incident of abuse**. This could take place in many forms, which will be discussed in more detail in a later section. The abusive incident could be a direct insult, a sarcastic joke, or a denial of a fact. The abusive incidents tend to become more intense or frequent over time.

After the incident, there are different **manipulative reactions** that may occur. Depending on the incident and on the victim's reaction, the abuser can behave in different ways. If an abusive incident happens privately between the couple, then it is very likely that when confronted by the victim, the abuser will flat out deny the abuse ('I don't know what you're talking about; I would never say something like that to you'). The victim may hear again that they are overly sensitive. The abuser will use words to explain his behavior and minimize the abusive incident. They may say something to the victim like, 'it really wasn't that big of a deal,' or 'it was just a joke.' Another path that the abuser may choose to take, especially if the incident did not have any outside witnesses, is to blame the victim. They will twist the incident around and say that it was the victim's fault that abuse happened. A very common phrase heard when an abuser chooses this path is, 'you made me angry/upset me, and that is why I said that.' It must be said again, that verbal abuse, and abuse of any kind, is never the victim's fault.

Another way in which the abuser might behave after an abusive incident is to apologize profusely. Abusers are concerned about preserving their ego and what they want. This means that they will take any manipulative measures necessary to 'fix' their relationship after an abusive incident. Whether or not the abuser is conscious of their manipulative behavior, is not of matter to the victim. Partners of abusers must be aware that the profuse apology is likely just a fear reaction on the part of the abuser. The abuser sees that they have really upset and/or angered the victim, and they fear that they may lose them. This fear reaction can provoke big portrayals of emotion and immense apologetic behaviors. After an especially dynamic abusive incident, the abuser may start to cry and express their regret. This is one way of confusing the victim by making them feel that the abusive behavior was an accidental outburst by the abuser. Abusers are generally very good with words and are able to make their victims sympathize with them. Another confusing aspect of being verbally abused in a relationship is that the abuser will often apologize abundantly. This confuses the victim into thinking that the abuser is honest with them and does what is right by apologizing for their negative behaviors. This makes victims more likely to forgive and rationalize the behavior of their abusive partner.

In addition to apologizing, many abusers will follow an abusive incident by bringing the victim gifts. The abuser may bring the victim something they really love after the incident or take them somewhere that they have been wanting to go. This is intended to pacify the victim and to confuse them into forgiving the abuser and moving forward with them. After an abusive incident, and during the subsequent manipulation phase of the abuse cycle, the abuser will almost always make empty promises. They will promise that the incident was a one-time mistake, they will promise to change their thought and behavior patterns, they will promise almost anything in order to satisfy the victim enough to move on from the incident. Needless to say, these promises are not to be believed or trusted.

The next phase of the cycle begins when the abuser has successfully manipulated the victim into forgiving the abuse, or at least agreeing to continue moving forward together as a couple. This is a phase that is often reminiscent of the beginning of the relationship. It is a **romantic fantasy** phase. The length of this phase can greatly vary due to the specific relationship and intensity level of the regular verbal abuse. During this phase, the victim has tricked themselves into believing that the relationship actually has a real chance to be healed, and move forward without any further abuse. The abuser spends time reestablishing the victim's trust during this stage. They will be on their best behavior and will compromise themselves much more than usual. They will often express the feeling of loving only the victim and wanting no one else. The victim may hear things from their partner like, 'I can't imagine my life without you,' or 'You are the only person who truly understands me,' during this phase. This is obviously very confusing for the victim because they are hearing the same kinds of things that led them to fall in love with their partner at the beginning of the relationship. However, this is a standard phase of the abuse cycle, and victims must be aware of the context of the relationship when they hear these things from their abusive partner.

As the fantasy phase inevitably comes to an end, the next phase, which proceeds the imminent next abusive incident, begins. This is the phase where the victim feels as if they are '**walking on eggshells**,' as the saying goes. The victim begins to feel the difference in dynamic again, as it changes from the theatrical fantasy phase. When the victim realizes that the abuser is no longer going out of their way to please them, care for them, and express their love, they begin to feel a persisting anxiety. The abuser's mood will likely change, and it becomes all about keeping them satisfied. The victim finds themselves using most of their energy thinking about how to avoid provoking an 'explosion' by the abuser. The victim cannot provoke abuse, although they feel this way. The abuser is responsible for their abusive behaviors. This phase is characterized by a palpable tension in the air, surrounding the abuser, and existing between the victim and abuser. There is no guideline to how long this phase lasts. Abusers are volatile, and their moods can change rapidly.

Another abusive incident marks the end of the tension phase and begins the cycle anew.

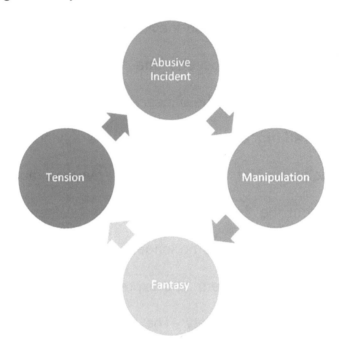

Chart 1

What Verbal Abuse Looks Like

Language is something very subjective. This makes it confusing for many to have clear ideas about what constitutes verbal abuse. It is clear, however, and there are many types of verbal abuse that one may encounter within a relationship. It is very important to be aware of different forms of verbal abuse, and how they feel. That way they are identifiable during the experience within a relationship. Having the knowledge of the range of verbal abuse provides defensive armor against manipulation attempts of the abuser.

All verbal abuse is not intense and obvious. There are many forms of abuse that are extremely subtle, and may not even be initially registered by the victim themselves. Due to interacting factors such as society and family values, many victims have internalized a belief system that convinces them that various types of verbal abuse are norms within relationships. The problem is that it does not matter if you believe it is a norm or not. The psychological effects of verbal abuse are extremely damaging to the victims. So it is better to deconstruct the beliefs that these types of abuse are norms so that victims can seek help and heal themselves.

The table below lists and explains some of the most common forms of verbal abuse that take place between couples:

Anger/Yelling/Shouting	Screaming, shouting, or yelling of any kind is verbal abuse. There is never a reason to scream/yell/shout at others. **Ex. 'SHUT UP!'**
Denial	The abuser denies that any of their remarks/behavior are abusive; denies/does not take responsibility for bad behavior. Rationalizes abusive behavior. **Ex. 'I yelled at you because you weren't listening to me.'**
Discounting	The abuser denies the victim's right to their own thoughts/feelings. The abuser consistently tells the victim they are overreactive or overly sensitive. Abuser denies victim's inner reality.

	Ex. 'Don't be so sensitive, try to take a joke!'
Trivializing/Undermining	The abuser trivializes/undermines aspects of the victim's life such as work, clothes, opinions. Purposely undermines things the victim says/does. Makes the victim question their own beliefs/interests/opinions. **Ex. 'Why would you wear that shirt? It's such an ugly color.'**
Abusive Jokes/Sarcasm	The abuser says things that are very hurtful and explains them as jokes. Mean comments disguised as sarcasm. **Ex. 'You'll be a great bank teller since you're SO good at math.'**
Name Calling	The abuser can call the outright victim names, such as 'bitch' or 'stupid.' It can also be subtle. **Ex. 'You think you're so special, don't you?'**
Countering	The abuser argues with almost everything the victim says on a regular

	basis. They purposely take the opposite stance from the victim in order to upset them and invalidate their feelings/opinions. **Ex. 'I don't know why you liked that movie, the acting was terrible.'**
Withholding/Blocking/Divertin g	The abuser does not engage in real conversation with the victim. Does not validate victim's feelings/opinions/ideas. Talks/answers in short/factual sentences. Tries to control topics of conversation by blocking/diverting. **Ex. 'You're complaining too much; taxes are set fees.'**
Blaming and Accusing	The abuser makes unwarranted accusations of the victim. Blames victim for things outside of their control. **Ex. 'My boss didn't promote me because you drank too much at the company dinner.'**
Criticizing and Judging	The abuser makes negative comments about the victim's

	character.
	Ex. 'You're lazy, and that's why you don't get promoted.'
Ordering	The abuser orders/demands that the victim says/behaves in certain ways. Abusive, emotional control. **Ex. 'This house is a mess, wash the dishes now!'**
Threatening	The abuser threatens the victim with actions or consequences. Can be direct or subtle. **Ex. 'If you're not careful of what you say to me, everyone will find out what kind of person you really are.'**

Table 1

A person experiencing any of these things in their relationship is being verbally abused. These forms of verbal abuse are not societal or familial norms, and they cannot be rationalized. Verbal abuse is legitimate, and the psychological effects are real.

It is likely that victims of verbal abuse will be subject to more than one form of abuse. The above list can present itself in any combination within a verbally abusive relationship. When verbal abuse is the combination of more than one type, it is more severe and can feel even more confusing for the victim. Different types of verbal abuse seem to contradict each other, and the abuser is able to create an atmosphere in which the victim is never sure which type of abuse to expect. This disables the victim and leaves them vulnerable to more intense and prolonged abuse because they are disoriented and unable to think quickly enough about a reasonable solution.

One of the most difficult parts of the healing process for the victims of verbal abuse is the first part, which is accepting that they have been abused by a person they love and once trusted. Recognizing the different types of verbal abuse in their own relationship can be a transformative moment for victims, in which they choose to seek help from others with their abusive experience. Victims of verbal abuse often wonder what changed about their partner, and why they changed? It often takes time for the victim to understand that their partner's change was never their fault. The abuser will behave in the same ways with any partner they're with. Victims hold no fault in their experience of abuse.

What happened to the loving partner?

The most important thing for victims of verbal abuse to know is that they could not have changed their partner's abusive behaviors by altering their own behavior. It will be difficult to separate from the abuser, but it is essential that the victim do so, at least to some extent. After recognizing the patterns of verbal abuse, victims often find themselves asking what happened to the person they had fallen in love with.

The reality of the situation can be hard to understand. Abusers present themselves in an ideal light at the beginning of any relationship. They behave in ways and say things that match their partner's fantasies about a relationship. The victim of verbal abuse needs to know that the person they saw at the beginning of their relationship was never the actual person they entered a companionship with.

The idealistic ways in which the abuser behaved were nothing more than a strong act through which they were able to achieve what they wanted, which was control in the relationship. Although even the abusers themselves are sometimes not aware of this drive within themselves, it is hidden deep, and directing their behaviors. The true nature of the abusive partner in a relationship is that which they show once the trust has been established and they feel that they are in controlling. So although it is hurtful for victims to accept, the real nature of their partner is much closer to the abusive person they have grown to know.

Understanding and accepting this can prove difficult, as the victims love their partners, despite the abuse they have experienced. They love the vulnerability and intimacy that they built at the beginning of the relationship and have spent the endurance of the abuse convincing themselves that the intimacy is the real aspect, not the abuse. Learning that it is actually the other way around, and working to accept that is a process of grieving.

In order to make space for the new understanding of their partner, the victim must grieve who they thought they were in a relationship with. They must spend time thinking about who they thought their partner was, and assure themselves that this was not their true nature, but a convincing act. They must use their courage to readjust to the new reality of their relationship and their partner's identity.

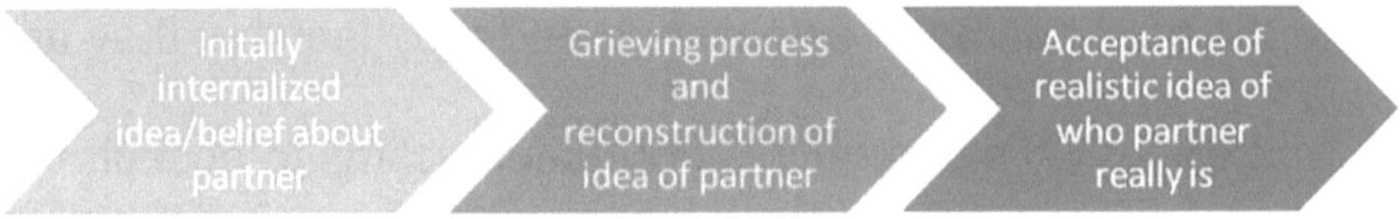

| Initally internalized idea/belief about partner | Grieving process and reconstruction of idea of partner | Acceptance of realistic idea of who partner really is |

Chart 2

Forgiveness in the Relationship

For the sake of the victim's wellbeing, it is ideal if they are able to work on choosing to forgive their partner. Forgive them for the lies they presented at the beginning of the relationship and forgive them for all of the hurt which they have caused. It is important to remember that forgiving does not mean forgetting or excusing.

By choosing to forgive their abusive partner, the victim is not expressing that the abuse they suffered was warranted or even justifiable. By choosing forgiveness, the victim is allowing themselves the chance to heal fully. Forgiveness of the abusive partner, allows the victim to change the way they think about their experience. They will not forget the abuse they experienced, and they will not condone it either, but they will not let the abuse and its effects control their lives. By forgiving, the victim frees themselves from the chains of their own memories and negative feelings about the abuse. They will be able to let go of the need to hold on to the suffering or 'victim' mindset and be able to take control of their lives once again.

Regardless of whether the victim of abuse chooses to leave the relationship or to stay in it, it is essential that they focus some of their energy on forgiving their abusive partner, so they will be able to move forward, unburdened into the next chapter of their lives.

Changing the Relationship with the Self

The effects of verbal abuse are heavy, and victims may not even realize how they have been affected until they identify and accept that they are in fact being abused. Being abused can have a lasting effect on belief systems and on how the victim relates to themselves. This is usually the most harmful effect of verbal abuse.

When the victim realizes that they are being abused and begins the process of grieving who they thought their partner was and forgiving them, they will be ready to begin reconstructing their relationship with themselves. The biggest secret to any successful relationship between two people, whether they are overcoming the effects of abuse or not, is that each individual must have a healthy relationship with themselves. What does it mean to have a healthy relationship with oneself?

This is a question that is pondered by all, at some point or another. The important thing to is love and care for oneself. To treat oneself as a close friend. One excellent way of relating to oneself that can be built with practice, over time, is self-compassion. With self-compassion, the victim of verbal abuse works on shifting their self-judgment and criticism to self-kindness and mindfulness.

The pursuit of increased self-compassion is a worthwhile one for victims of verbal abuse, as they have likely constructed a very cruel inner voice as a result of the abuse. Practicing self-compassion will help them to realize that this voice inside of them is not telling them the truth. It is a result of being abused by another person who was not able to love themselves. With continued practice of self-compassion, victims of verbal abuse will be able to rebuild their sense of self and find confidence in their beliefs, feelings, ideas, and opinions once again. Self-compassion provides the added benefit of helping the victims manage negative experiences and emotions in a healthier way, going forward. While they may have become extremely negative or overly critical of themselves as a result of the abuse, self-compassion will help them work to have a more realistic and balanced perspective of themselves and situations they encounter.

A simple, but deeply effective way to practice self-compassion is by thinking of oneself as a younger self. To imagine oneself as a four or five-year-old version is extremely transformative. It also helps to look at a picture of oneself from childhood in order to make it easier to think in that way. Remembering how one would talk to a child is a quick way to get back on track when critical self-talk emerges, as a result of verbal abuse.

Why Focus on the Self if the Fault is with the Abuser?

Though the abuse is never the fault of the victim, it is the responsibility of the victim to choose how they respond. The fact is that there will be psychological damage as an effect of verbal abuse. The victim must remember, however, that they are in charge of how they choose to deal with that damage, and how they choose to approach healing.

Choosing to focus on the self, is choosing to be proactive in the healing process. When an abuse victim focuses on their self, they are opening a world to themselves in which they can develop deeper self-awareness, which can lead to many things such as clearer boundaries and deeper self-respect.

Healing begins with the self. It begins with choosing to take responsibility and control over one's reactions, both emotional and behavioral. Victims can feel empowered by this focus on their self, after having spent so much energy trying to appease their abusive partner. The reality is the no one can control another, and the sooner victims of verbal abuse stop compromising themselves to try to control the abusive situation, the sooner they can begin to work on improving themselves, which will lead to improved overall health and wellbeing.

Seeking Support

The initial difficulty of accepting the reality of abuse will eventually subside. When the victim accepts that they are in fact being verbally abused, it is vital that they choose to reach out instead of pulling into themselves. The first instinct of a victim of verbal abuse may be to keep the abuse a secret. There are many feelings that come along with being the victim of verbal abuse, which can include embarrassment and shame. These feelings will try to tell the victim that it is best to keep the abuse a secret, but this is a lie of a warped belief system.

Verbal abuse must not be kept secret. Victims may feel scared to take big steps towards help, like telling family, or mutual friends of the victim and the abuser, but it is necessary that the victim seeks support somewhere. Whether support from a friend at work, an exercise class, or even through an online forum, victims must find private places and outside people with whom to talk about their experience of verbal abuse.

The reason that it is so integral to the victim's wellbeing is because when they confide in outside sources, victims will be given a realistic perspective on the situation. While the victim themselves may have construed the idea that they deserve this treatment, the outside sources will be able to identify the situation as abusive. Even if this does not prompt action in the victim, it is important for keeping them grounded in reality.

People experiencing verbal abuse and seeking support must remain aware and vigilant about whose 'support' they take. Sometimes, victims may confide in people who will actually reinforce the practice of verbal abuse. These people may have grown up in situations where verbal abuse was condoned as a norm, and may simply not know any better. This type of support may sound something like, 'I understand that it's difficult to hear those things, but he's telling you because he wants what is best for you.' Misguided support can be dangerous and reinforce the victim's mindset of helplessness.

Positive support is that which reflects the reality of the situation back to the abused. A positive support system will remind the victim that they are an individual worthy of sharing their ideas, whose feelings are valid. At the very least, a positive support system will provide the victim of verbal abuse with a safe space to work out their feelings about their experience with the abuse.

Providing support for someone who is experiencing or has experienced verbal abuse can be difficult. Things that seem black and white to the supporter may be hard to distinguish for the victim. The supporter must be able to empathize with the victim and understand that their perspective is confused and clouded. While suggesting solutions to the victim is a reasonable idea for the supporter, it can sometimes backfire. Victims of abuse are particularly sensitive to feeling that others are trying to push their views or wants on them. For that reason, people providing support to victims of verbal abuse must be mindful and willing to work with the victim at their own pace. This may mean supporting them while they remain in an abusive relationship because they are not emotionally ready to leave. Providing support to

abuse victims is a delicate process, and is just as vital as a

victim asking for support.

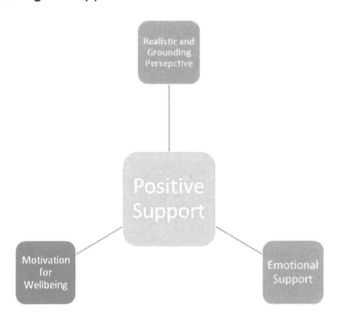

Chart 3

Confronting the Abuser

When a person being verbally abused comes to realize the situation they are in and receives some outside perspective and support; they may start to feel as if they want to confront their abusive partner. In their minds, this may seem reasonable, as the image of their partner at the beginning of the relationship is still in their memory. The reality, however, is that confronting an abuser is a very tricky and potentially dangerous situation. The victim needs to go about the confrontation in the best way possible, in order to protect themselves.

When an emotional and verbal abuser is confronted, it can quickly escalate to a reaction of physical violence. This is because the abuser will feel that their ego is in danger, and that threat will lead them to try to take control of the situation in a clearer and firmer way. This is why it is important that people who want to confront their abusers do not do it rashly.

The act of confrontation at all may not be the best tactic in trying to stop the verbal abuse in a relationship. The only effective way to stop abuse is for the victim to change the ways in which they react to the abuse. This is not putting the responsibility of the abuse on the victim, but rather empowering them with the ability to assert stronger boundaries.

Instead of being emotionally pulled into the abuse and reacting with fear, victims should practice setting a clear boundary in the moment of abuse. When their partner begins a verbally abusive incident, the victim can attempt a calm confrontation by saying 'Stop,' firmly, but in an even tone. However, if this does not help the situation to subside, then the victim must set a clear boundary and walk away. Removing themselves from the situation may save the victims from an extra abuse. It also may allow the abuser space to calm down.

It is important for the victim to set some kind of boundary in moments of abuse. Whether it is firmly telling the abuser to stop, leaving the situation, or simply refusing to engage, the victim needs to maintain control of their reaction.

Deciding Whether to Stay or Leave the Relationship

Each relationship is unique, even when they involve verbal abuse. That is why there is no standard answer as to how decided whether it is best to stay or leave a verbally abusive relationship. This is something that must not be determined lightly and should be given an adequate amount of thought and consideration.

There are many practical factors that play a role in a victim's decision to leave or stay in an abusive relationship. These may include financial dependency or children in the relationship. Sometimes because of different factors, the decision about whether to stay or leave is not as clear as it may seem to an outsider. A person who has never been verbally abused may assert that they would leave immediately the first time they were verbally abused. However, it is much different to imagine a situation than to live it. By the time the abuse occurs, and the victims grasp the reality of their situation, life is often tied into their relationships. They feel that there is more at stake than their wellbeing.

For example, a young woman entered a relationship with a young man. In the beginning, all was wonderful, they were in love and decided to move in together. Within a month of moving in together, the young woman became pregnant. The pregnancy was a dream come true for the young woman, and she was overjoyed with what the future of her family would hold. The young man surprised the woman when his initial reaction was not as enthusiastic as hers, but she decided that she still wanted to move ahead and marry him.

A few months into the pregnancy, the young couple was married, and the young woman was excitedly awaiting the arrival of her first child. Suddenly, she began to notice changes in the way her husband treated her. He began to lose his temper, shouting at his wife when the dishes were left in the sick at night. The young woman, confused, told herself that her husband was simply stressed about making enough money to provide for their new baby. As time went on, however, her husband began to verbally abuse her in other ways. He blamed her for their financial struggles, saying that if she had not gotten pregnant, then he would not have to work extra hours at his job. He made 'jokes' about her maternity clothes, and told her that he no longer recognized her at this weight. The young woman was emotionally distraught and shocked. She did not understand why her loving husband had turned his back on her and become so cruel. She felt that all she could was rationalize his behavior as being due to stress. He was the father of her child.

The baby was born, and the young woman hoped and tricked herself into believing that her husband's 'stress' would lessen, and he would once again become the doting and supportive partner he once was. Instead, the verbal abuse escalated. He withheld any real interaction and began calling her sarcastic names, like 'trophy wife,' as a comment on her struggle to lose her baby weight.

By this time, the young woman began to share her experience with a friend, a fellow new mom, in hopes of sharing their stories of their husbands' stress. However, her friend ended up being her support system, as she told her that the verbal abuse she was experiencing was not normal or due to stress. As she grew to better understand her situation, the woman felt torn. She did not want to compromise her self-worth and deal with her husband's continued denial of abuse, but she also did not want her child to grow up without its father, which was her husband's main controlling threat.

This is an example of how fragile and complicated the decision can be about whether to stay in or leave abusive relationships. In order to make a healthy decision, victims of verbal abuse would be best suited to seek professional help. With therapy, people experiencing verbal abuse with being able to reestablish a balanced perspective of reality, and will be able to analyze the pros and cons of each side of their pending decision.

Cognitive Behavioral Therapy

Perhaps the most effective type of therapy for a person is being or has been verbally abused is Cognitive Behavioral Therapy (CBT). CBT is a very common form of therapy, which combines talk and analytical therapy with structured behavior modification. In CBT, people work on reconstructing their negative thoughts and behaviors, into more positive patterns.

A victim of verbal abuse who goes for CBT will be guided by the therapist to talk about their experience. When looking at their experience, they will spend time searching for the effects that the abuse has left in the victim's thinking pattern. The victim and the therapist will work to identify and separate the victim's critical and judging inner voice from their loving one. While doing this work, the therapist will help the victim to understand that the ways they are thinking about themselves are effects of the abuse they endured. They will work together to retrain the victim's brain to understand that the abuse was not their fault, but that they are not helpless, either.

When specific thought patterns and belief systems that the victim wants to work on have been identified, the therapist and victim will work together in constructing a plan through which to alter these thoughts and their subsequent behaviors. This plan may include things such as daily journaling, practicing asking for help, or even practicing self-compassion meditations. The goals of the therapist and the victim will always focus on the increased wellbeing of the victim and move away from the effects of the verbal abuse.

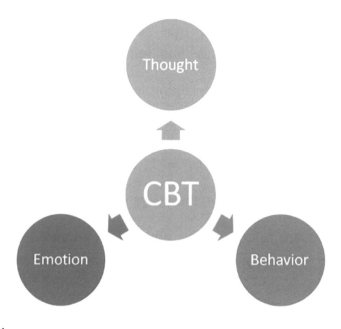

Chart 4

Can an Abuser Change?

The question of whether or not an abuser can truly change is a tricky one. It is dependent on many factors. First and foremost, it must be noted that an abuser, or any person for that matter, can change only when they want to. No other person can force another to change. Ultimatums do not make people change. A person can and will change only if and when they choose to. That being said, if an abuser does want to change, they will need to do some serious work.

Just as a victim of verbal abuse must make the choice to change their reactions to abuse, an abuser must make the choice to change their reactions to stress and frustration. In order to change their abusive behavior, an abuser will first need to identify why they behave in that way. This means digging deep to uncover possible past trauma and to recognize dysfunctional ways of thinking.

Just like victims need help to reconstruct, so do abusers. While it is not an excuse for their behavior, most abusers have previously been victims of abuse themselves. They have internalized their experience and learned to relate with the world in this way. Abusers also need to attend CBT in order to work on restructuring their thought processes and creating healthy ways to deal with their frustrations.

If an abuser chooses to seek help and attend CBT, then there is definitely a chance that they can change. That being said, abusers have intricate thought patterns which have been reinforced enough to create maladaptive behavior patterns. So this means that it will take them quite some time to fully change their abusive tendencies if they are truly motivated to do so.

Changing the Dynamic of the Relationship

If the abuser and the victim both choose and agree to seek separate treatment to work on themselves, then there may be a chance that they will be able to salvage their relationship. This is something that would need to be considered at a later date when both individuals had spent time working on themselves.

A relationship which had abuse is one that did not begin in full honesty, as the abuser was not able to show themselves for they really were, and later began abusing their partner. This means that the trust in an abusive relationship will be extremely damaged and may be irreparable.

It is first the choice of the victim of the verbal abuse if they are interested in trying to repair the relationship. Whether there are things at stake such as shared children or financial ties may affect this decision, but it should be based mainly on the emotional and psychological state of the victim. If the victim does feel that they would like to try to move forward with the relationship than it is imperative that the couple finds a joint therapist. It is preferable if the couple seeks a different therapist than the ones they have been seeing individually. This is to eliminate any resentment from either side when the therapist makes decisive statements about either party.

In couple's therapy, the duo will need to focus on rebuilding a sense of fair trust. This means that the abuser will need to present themselves to the victim transparently, in order for the victim to feel safe enough to try to trust them again. After establishing a foundation of trust, the couple will be able to explore each other as if dating for the first time. It will feel safer for the previous victim to spend the beginning of the new phase of the relationship monitored and refereed by a couple's therapist.

Moving on After a Verbally Abusive Relationship

Many times, it is not worth it for the victim to try to salvage the relationship with their abusive partner. When this is the case, the victim must learn how to create a new path for themselves following their experience of abuse. This can feel daunting.

Even with therapy and support, people who have experienced verbal abuse can find themselves feeling emotionally raw and vulnerable when they try to move on. They may find that they have heightened anxiety or depression. They may find themselves crying more than usual and having difficulty making even small decisions. This is a normal part of the transition back into themselves. It is a painful and demanding process, however.

In order to move on healthily after experiencing abuse, a person has to really spend a lot of time working on themselves. They must work to find and identify the things within themselves that led them to engage with an abuser. Often times, victims of verbal abuse discover that they had internalized patterns from childhood that they were not even fully aware of. Perhaps they had witnessed regular verbal abuse between their parents, or perhaps they had even been a childhood victim of verbal abuse. Whatever it is, they must find the obstacles within themselves in order to move towards wellbeing.

The journey of the person who has left a verbally abusive relationship becomes that of learning to truly love themselves. Their mission becomes the job of loving themselves fully before sharing themselves with another person again. Their experience with verbal abuse can give them further insight into themselves and the way they interact with the rest of the world. If they choose to view the abuse as a learning experience, they can develop greater resilience as a result.

Concluding Remarks

Verbal abuse is not something to be taken lightly. Although many abusers themselves, even high profile ones, try to undermine the severity of this form of abuse, it cannot be undermined. Various studies in recent years have highlighted and proven the fact that verbal abuse produces the same psychological effects, sometimes worse and longer lasting effects, as physical abuse. This is a phenomenon to pay attention to and to face head on.

Victims of verbal abuse know that it is not a lighter form of abuse than physical abuse, but actually an even more demented type, which leaves the victim completely disoriented in their own life. The identifiable types of verbal abuse must be taught widely to people of all ages, in order to prevent victims suffering without need. It is important that all people be aware of what verbal abuse is. If a person witnesses verbal abuse, they should step in to try and help the victim. In order for that to be effective, however, there needs to be a widespread knowledge so as to create a shield of support for victims.

People who have suffered from verbal abuse do not have to feel doomed. Learned helplessness is reversible with proper therapy. There is no reason that people must go their whole lives feeling scared and vulnerable after being the victim of verbal abuse. It must be a global mission to work on reintroducing a sense of self-worth and value to victims of verbal abuse. They must feel supported, heard, and understood by those around them.

The most responsible thing to do when facing verbal abuse is to seek help. Victims and witnesses of verbal abuse must be willing to use their courage to speak up, share their story, and ask others to help them. By speaking up about verbal abuse, the stigma is slowly destroyed. As the stigma is destroyed, it makes it much harder to for abusers to behave in secret. Being a victim of verbal abuse is nothing to be ashamed of, and there is only positivity to be gained from confiding in others about the experience. Encourage a wider spread conversation about verbal abuse!

Appendix

1. Abuse of a Different Nature

2. The Abusers

3. The Subtle Beginning to Abuse

4. The Cycle of Abuse

    a. Chart 1

5. What Verbal Abuse Looks Like
    a. Table 1: Types of Verbal Abuse

6. What happened to the loving partner?

    a. Chart 2

7. Forgiveness in the Relationship

8. Changing the Relationship with the Self

9. Why Focus on the Self if the Fault is with the

    Abuser?

10. Seeking Support

    a. Chart 3

11. Confronting the Abuser

12. Deciding Whether to Stay or Leave the Relationship

13. Cognitive Behavioral Therapy

    a. Chart 4

Your Free Gift

I wanted to show my appreciation that you support my work so I've put together a free gift for you.

http://www.olkha.co/gelato.html

Just visit the link above to download it now.

I know you will love this gift.

Thanks!

If you enjoyed this book, do not forget to leave a review on Amazon! I highly appreciate your reviews, and it only takes a minute to do.

Welcome to visit my other books If you want to get fun educational stories for your children!!!

https://www.amazon.com/dp/B06ZZS98R3

Made in United States
Troutdale, OR
08/29/2023